Customs, Arts and Entertainment

An Inca funeral procession

Once the necessities of survival were mastered, people could turn their attention to spiritual and creative matters. In this section you will discover that many artefacts and customs were inspired by religious beliefs and rituals. You will also find early versions of sports, games, toys and entertainment that are still enjoyed by people today.

Arts and Crafts

N o other species on the Earth has shown the ability to express itself in the same artistic way as humans. Archaeological evidence has shown that, over 50,000 years ago, the earliest humans decorated their bodies, tools and shelters with simple patterns and symbols. People then began to portray the world around them by painting images on the walls of caves. As society evolved, so did the art and culture. This is charted in history – from the early treasures of the Egyptian tombs, through the Golden Age of Greek art and Roman architecture, to the Renaissance – the revival of art and culture that formed the transition from the Middle Ages to our modern world.

▲ Cave paintings
Paintings of animals made more than 17,000 years ago have been found painted on the walls deep inside caves in Europe. They often show animals that were hunted at that time.

▲ Horse of stone
An early Egyptian stone carving of a horse's head, dating from around 1500BC. In Egyptian society, skilled artists and craftworkers formed a middle class between the poor labourers and rich officials and nobles.

◄ Skilled ironworkers
Metalworkers were some of the most important members of Celtic society. They made many of the items that Celtic people valued most, such as this magnificent iron axe head. It took many years for a metalworker to learn all the necessary skills, first to produce the metal from nuggets or lumps of ore, and then to shape it.

▲ Buried treasures

This Greek wine serving bowl, or krater, was found in a wood-lined burial chamber at Vix in eastern France. The tomb belonged to a Celtic princess, who was buried around 520BC. The princess was wearing a torc, or necklace, made of almost half a kilogram of pure gold.

Monster watch ▶

The entrance to an Assyrian palace in Mesopotamia was guarded by statues of huge monsters called lamassus. Lamassus were strange creatures with the bodies of lions or bulls, the wings of mighty birds, human heads and caps to show they had divine powers. Lamassus had five legs. The extra limb was so that they did not appear one-legged if seen from the front.

◀ Tomb horse

By the 3rd century AD, Japan was governed by a culture known as the Yamato. When a Yamato emperor died, his huge burial tomb was filled with armour, jewellery and weapons to indicate his great power and wealth. People surrounded his burial site with thousands of pottery objects, such as this horse. They were meant to protect the tomb and its contents.

Stone warrior ▶

This statue of a proud warrior stood at Tula, the ancient capital city of the Toltec people. The Toltecs were rulers of northern Mexico from about AD950 to 1160. The warrior wears a butterfly-shaped breastplate. Butterflies have short but brilliant lives. For the Toltecs, they were a symbol of brave warriors and early death.

Stone Age hand art

From about 37,000BC, early humans began to carve marks on bones and use pebbles to count. Days may have been counted on calendar sticks. Experts have noticed dots and symbols in some cave paintings, which may be counting tallies or the very beginnings of a writing system. By 7000BC, tokens with symbols to represent numbers and objects were being used by traders in the Near East. Such tokens may have led to the first written script. This developed in about 3100BC and was a form of picture-writing called cuneiform.

YOU WILL NEED

Self-hardening clay, rolling pin, cutting board, modelling tool, fine sandpaper, red and yellow acrylic paints, water, two spray bottles.

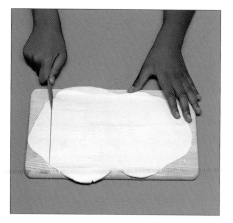

1 Roll out a piece of clay. Make sure it has an uneven surface similar to a cave wall. Use a modelling tool to trim the edges into a rough rectangle to look like a stone tablet.

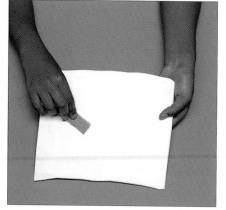

2 Leave the clay to dry. When the tablet is completely hard, rub it with fine sandpaper to get rid of any sharp edges and to make a smooth surface for your cave painting.

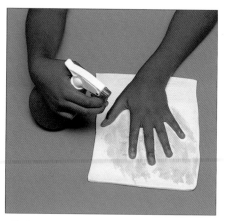

3 Mix the yellow paint with some water and fill a spray bottle. Mix the red paint in the same way. Put one hand on top of the clay tablet and spray plenty of yellow paint around it.

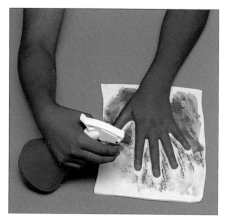

4 Keeping your hand in exactly the same position, spray on the red paint from the other bottle. Make sure you spray enough paint to leave a clear, sharp background.

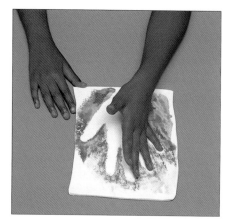

5 When you have finished your spray painting, carefully remove your hand. Take care not to smudge the paint, and then leave the tablet to dry. Wash your hands thoroughly.

This project is based on a Stone Age painting found in a cave in Argentina. The original artist blew paint through a reed or even spat paint on to the wall.

Stone Age cave painting

The earliest Stone Age cave paintings date from around 40,000BC and were etched on rocks in Australia. In Europe, the oldest works of art are cave paintings from about 28,000BC. Some caves in southwestern France and northern Spain are covered with paintings and engravings of animals, but show very few human figures. They were probably part of religious rituals. Stone Age artists also carved female figures, called Venus figurines, and decorated their tools and weapons with carved patterns and animal forms.

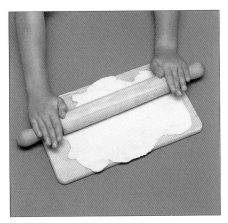

1 Roll out a piece of clay. Make sure it has an uneven surface similar to a cave wall. Then use a modelling tool to trim the edges into a neat rectangle shape.

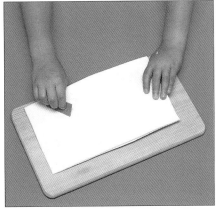

2 Leave the clay to dry. When it is completely hard, rub it with fine sandpaper to get rid of any sharp edges and to make a smooth surface for your painting.

3 Paint the outline of an animal, such as this reindeer, using black acrylic paint. Exaggerate the size of the most obvious features, such as the muscular body and antlers.

4 When the outline is dry, mix black, red and yellow acrylic paints to make a warm, earthy colour. Use the colour you have mixed to fill in the outline of your chosen animal.

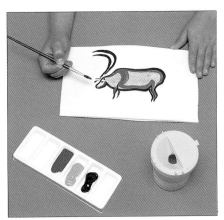

5 Finish your painting by highlighting some parts of the animal's body with reddish brown paint mixed to resemble red ochre. This is how Stone Age artists finished their paintings.

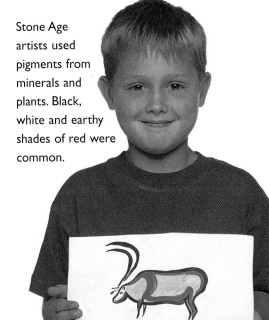

Stone Age artists used pigments from minerals and plants. Black, white and earthy shades of red were common.

Egyptian wall painting

The walls of many Egyptian tombs were covered with colourful pictures, which were very carefully made. First, the wall was coated several times with plaster. Then it was marked out in a grid pattern to make sure that each part of the design fitted neatly into the available space. Junior artists sketched the picture in red paint. Senior artists made corrections and went over the outlines in black ink. Finally, the outlines were filled in with paint. The step-by-step panel below shows you how to draw figures the Egyptian way.

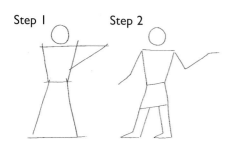
Step 1   Step 2

To draw figures without a grid, start with simple lines and circles. Then add simple lines for limbs and draw a tray on the shoulder. Round off the lines for the arms and legs.

Step 3

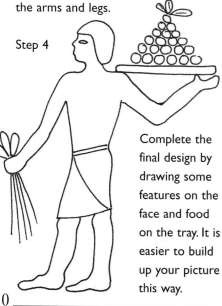
Step 4

Complete the final design by drawing some features on the face and food on the tray. It is easier to build up your picture this way.

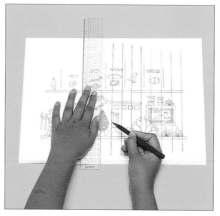

1 Draw a pencil design similar to the one shown in the final picture. Go over it with a black pen. Then use a red pen and ruler to draw vertical and horizontal lines in a 2cm-square grid.

3 Mix the plaster of Paris and water in a bowl using a wooden spoon. The plaster of Paris should have a firm consistency, and the mixture should drop from the spoon in thick dollops.

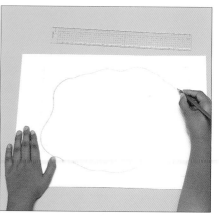

2 Measure the maximum length and maximum width of your design. Draw a rectangular box of the same size on a piece of card, and then draw a wavy shape inside the box.

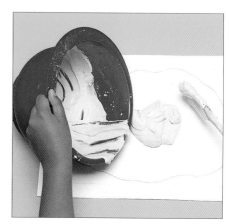

4 Smear a little petroleum jelly over the piece of card. This stops the plaster from sticking to the card. Then pour the plaster of Paris to cover the wavy shape you drew earlier.

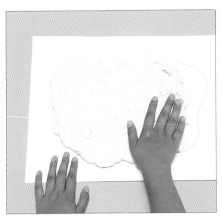

5 Spread the plaster mixture to a depth of about 8mm. Then smooth the surface with your hand. Leave this shape to dry in a warm room for at least two hours.

6 When it is dry, gently rub the plaster with coarse sandpaper. Smooth the sandpaper over the rough edges and all over the surface and sides of your slab of plaster.

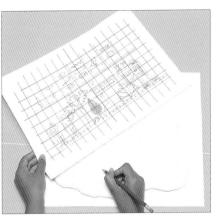

7 Use the ruler and pencil to draw another 2cm-square grid on the surface of the plaster. Carefully remove the piece of plaster from the card by lifting one edge at a time.

8 Transfer the design on the paper grid on to the plaster grid. Begin at the centre square and work outwards, copying one square at a time.

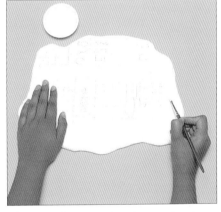

9 Use a fine paintbrush to paint the background of the plaster a cream colour. Then paint around the design itself. Leave the paint to dry for at least an hour before adding other colours.

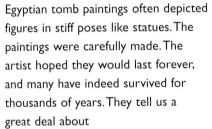

Egyptian tomb paintings often depicted figures in stiff poses like statues. The paintings were carefully made. The artist hoped they would last forever, and many have indeed survived for thousands of years. They tell us a great deal about how ancient Egyptians lived.

10 When the background is dry, add the details of the Egyptian painting using a fine paintbrush. Paint the border using red, blue, yellow, black, white and gold acrylic paints.

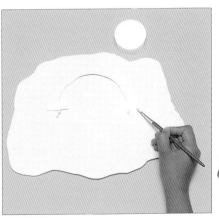

11 Tie a knot at each end of the piece of string. Cut two small pieces of fabric and glue them over the string as shown above. When the glue is dry, you can hang your painting.

Greek vase

The artists and craftworkers of ancient Greece were admired for the quality of their work. They used a range of materials, such as metals, stone, wood, leather, bone, horn and glass. Most goods were made on a small scale in workshops surrounding the *agora* (marketplace). A craftsman might work on his own or with the help of his family and a slave or two. In larger workshops, slaves laboured to produce bulk orders of popular goods. These might include shields, pottery and metalwork, all of which were traded around the Mediterranean Sea for a large profit.

▲ Work of art
A good vase painter was a highly respected artist, and many signed their works. The export of vases was a major source of income for Athens.

▶ Storage space
Huge storage jars were used by the ancient Greeks to store food and drink. One jar could contain hundreds of litres of wine, olive oil or cereal. Handmade from clay, they kept food and drink cool in the hot Mediterranean climate.

1 Blow up a balloon. Soak strips of newspaper in one part PVA glue to two parts water to make papier mâché. Cover the balloon with two layers of papier mâché. Leave it to dry.

2 Using a roll of masking tape as a guide, draw and cut out two holes at the top and bottom of the papier mâché balloon. Discard the burst balloon.

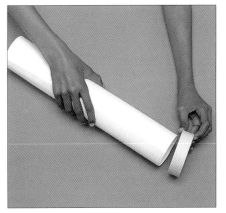

3 Roll the 42 x 30cm sheet of paper into a tube. Make sure it will fit through the middle of the roll of masking tape. Glue the paper tube in place and secure with masking tape.

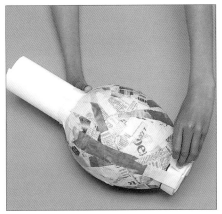

4 Push the tube through the middle of the papier mâché shape. Tape the tube into place. Push a roll of masking tape over the bottom of the paper tube and tape as shown above.

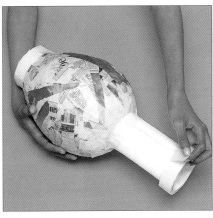

5 Attach the second roll of masking tape to the top of the paper tube. Make sure that both rolls of tape are securely fixed at either end of the paper tube.

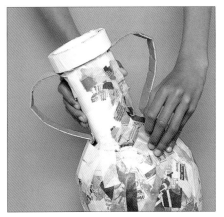

6 Cut two 15cm strips of card. Fix them to either side of the vase for handles as shown above. Cover the entire vase with more papier mâché and leave to dry. Paint the vase cream.

7 When dry, use a pencil to copy the pattern above, or design a simple geometric pattern like the pots on the left. Paint over the design in black acrylic paint. Leave the vase to dry.

Greek vases such as the one you have made were called amphorae. They were given out as prizes at the Panathenaic games and were decorated with sporting images.

Japanese ikebana

Although the word *ikebana* roughly translates as 'flower arrangement', the Japanese incorporate all sorts of other organic things in their designs. Driftwood, rocks and shells can all be brought into use. In an ikebana arrangement, the vase or pot represents the Earth, and the plants set in it should be arranged as if they are growing naturally.

This idea is carried through to Japanese gardens which are often small but create a miniature landscape. Each rock, pool or gateway is positioned where it forms part of a balanced and harmonious arrangement. Japanese designers create gardens that look good during all the different seasons of the year. Zen gardens sometimes have no plants at all – just rocks, sand and gravel.

▲ Tiny tree

Bonsai is the Japanese art of producing miniature, but perfectly formed, trees such as this maple. This is achieved by clipping the roots and branches of the tree and training it with wires.

◄ The art of elegance

Japanese flower arrangements are often very simple. Flowers have been appreciated in Japan for hundreds of years. In the 8th century AD, thousands of poems were collected together in one book. About a third of the poems were about plants and flowers.

YOU WILL NEED

Twig, scissors, vase filled with water, raffia or string, two flowers (one with a long stem; one shorter), branch of foliage, two stems of waxy leaves.

Cut the twig so that it can be wedged into the neck of the vase. The twig will provide a structure to build on and will also control the position of the flowers.

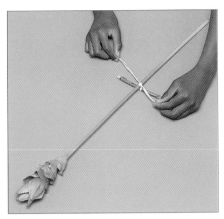

2 Remove the twig from the vase. Next, using a piece of string or raffia, tie the twig tightly on to the stem of the longest flower. Make the knot about halfway down the stem.

3 Place the flower stem in the vase. As you do this, gently slide the twig back into the neck of the vase so that it is wedged into the same position as it was before.

4 Add the flower with the shorter stem to the vase. Position this flower so that it slants forwards and to one side. Carefully lean this flower stem towards the longer one.

5 Slip the branch of foliage between the two stems. It should lean outwards and forwards. The foliage should look as if it is a naturally growing branch.

6 Position some waxy leaves at the neck of the vase. Ikebana is the arrangement of anything that grows, so the foliage is just as important as the flowers in your arrangement.

7 Add a longer stem of waxy leaves at the back of the vase to complete the arrangement, which is typical of the kinds that Japanese people use to decorate their homes.

The three main branches of this arrangement represent heaven, the Earth and human beings. Even the leaves and other material are arranged in a carefully balanced way.

Celtic manuscript

By around AD1, the Celtic lands of mainland Europe were part of the Roman Empire. Over the next 400 years, Celtic languages and artistic traditions were gradually absorbed into the Roman Empire.

In the British Isles, the situation was different, as they were more isolated and many parts were never conquered by Rome. Languages and traditions survived, creating a final flowering of Celtic culture, particularly in the Christian monasteries. There, the monks were making careful copies of sacred Christian texts. They decorated their manuscripts with plaited and spiralling Celtic designs in rich colours. In this way, the new and quite distinctive form of Celtic illumination was developed. Some manuscripts had notes scribbled in the margins such as "The ink is bad ... the day dark."

▲ Irish saint

A missionary called St Patrick took the Christian faith to Ireland. Irish monks made beautifully illuminated manuscripts. Their love of nature was obvious in their lively pictures of animals and birds.

▲ Beautiful border

The *Book of Durrow* is a Christian book decorated with Celtic designs. It was made on the Scottish island of Iona.

▲ Stone marker

Celtic standing stones were often turned into Christian crosses to mark burials, preaching places or holy ground.

1 Use a pen to draw a 57 x 37cm rectangle on the thin card. Draw lines 1cm in from the long sides and 1.5cm in from the short sides. Then draw lines 9.5cm in from each end.

2 Divide the border at the top of the card into two horizontal sections. Now mark vertical sections 3.5cm in from each end. Then add three more vertical lines 7cm apart.

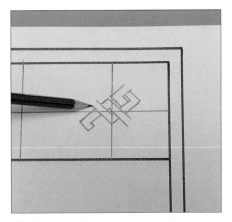

3 Begin at the top right-hand corner of the top section of the border. Place your pencil at the intersection of the first four squares. Draw a design similar to the one shown above.

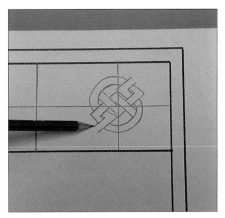

4 Add two outer circles to your design as shown above. Join the circles to the open ends of your Celtic border to create a design known as an endless knot.

5 Add two even larger circles and the corner designs to your endless knot as shown above. Extend the open ends on the left of the design to begin a second knot.

6 Create a row of endless knots. Repeat these steps to create an endless knot design in the border along the bottom of the card.

7 Paint the different strands of knot using typical Celtic colours, such as green and red. When the border is completely dry, carefully rub out the pencil grid.

You could write a few Gaelic words on to your manuscript. The words shown here mean 'And pray for Mac Craith, King of Cashell'. Interlaced designs such as this one are found in manuscripts decorated in Celtic style.

Inca tumi knife

The whole region of the Andes had a very long history of metalworking. Incas often referred to gold as 'sweat of the Sun' and to silver as 'tears of the Moon'. These metals were sacred to the gods and also to the Inca rulers and priests – the gods on Earth. At the Temple of the Sun in Cuzco, there was a whole garden made of gold and silver, with golden soil, golden stalks of maize and golden llamas. Imagine how it must have gleamed in the sunlight! Copper, however, was used by ordinary people. It was made into cheap jewellery, weapons and everyday tools. The Incas' love of gold and silver eventually led to their downfall, for it was rumours of their fabulous wealth that lured the Spanish to invade the region in the 1400s.

▲ **Copper ore**
The Incas worked with copper, found in rocks like this one, and knew how to mix it with tin to make bronze. The Incas also used gold, silver and platinum, but not iron or steel.

▲ **Tumi knife**
A ceremonial knife with a crescent-shaped blade is known as a tumi. Its gold handle is made in the shape of a ruler.

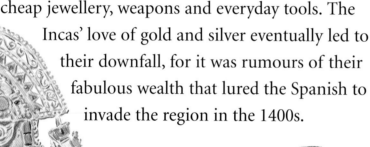

▲ **Precious blade**
The handle of this Inca sacrificial knife is made of wood inlaid with gemstones, shells and turquoise.

YOU WILL NEED

Card, pencil, ruler, scissors, self-hardening clay, cutting board, rolling pin, modelling tool, PVA glue and glue brush, toothpick, gold paint, paintbrush, water pot, blue metallic paper.

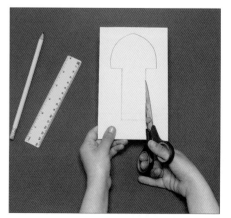

I Draw the shape of the knife blade on a piece of card and cut it out as shown above. The rectangular part measures 9 x 3.5cm. The rounded part is 7cm across and 4.5cm high.

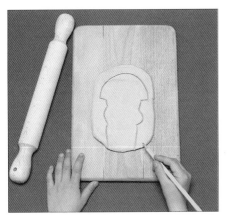

2 Roll out a slab of clay to a thickness of 1cm. Pencil in a tumi shape as shown above. It should be about 12.5cm long and measure 9cm across the widest part at the top.

3 Use the modelling tool to cut around the clay shape you have drawn. Put the leftover clay to one side. Make sure the edges of the tumi handle are clean and smooth.

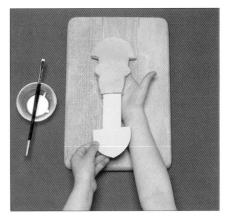

4 Use the modelling tool to cut a slot in the bottom edge of the tumi handle. Lifting it carefully, slide the card blade into the handle. Use glue to join the blade and the handle firmly.

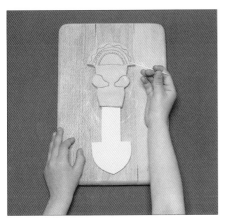

5 Use a modelling tool to mark on the details of the tumi. Use a toothpick for the fine details. Look at the finished knife (*right*) to see how to do this. Leave everything to dry.

6 When the clay is dry, give one side of the tumi and blade a coat of gold paint. Leave it to dry completely before turning it over and painting the other side.

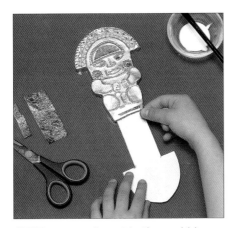

7 The original tumi knife would have been decorated with pieces of turquoise. Glue small pieces of blue metallic paper on to the handle for turquoise as shown in the picture.

The Chimú gold and turquoise tumi was used by priests of the Chimú people at religious ceremonies. It may even have been used to kill sacrifices to the gods.

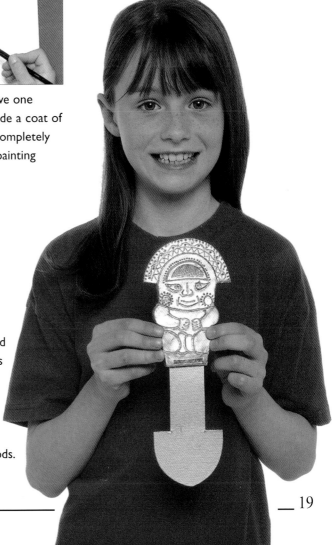

19

Customs

▲ Urn for ashes

In some ancient societies, people cremated their dead by burning the bodies on a funeral pyre. The ashes, and sometimes the bones, of the dead person were placed in pottery urns such as the one above. The urn was then placed in a burial chamber.

Today, many aspects of life are similar from one side of the world to the other. People wear the same sort of clothes, drive similar cars and live and work in the same sort of houses and apartment blocks. This has not always been the case. For thousands of years, customs and lifestyles varied greatly between different continents and even between countries and regions. There were differences in how people dressed, what they ate and how they greeted each other.

Many customs are very closely related to religion, such as Ramadan (a Muslim period of fasting) and the barmitzvah (a coming-of-age ceremony for Jewish boys). Some ancient customs are still practised today, but a great many have been forgotten and lost forever.

▲ Crying a river

Osiris was the Egyptian god of farming. After he was killed by his jealous brother, Seth, Osiris became a god of the underworld and the afterlife. The ancient Egyptians believed that the yearly flooding of the River Nile marked the anniversary of Osiris's death when his queen, Isis (*above*), wept for him.

Symbol of hope ▶

The water lily, or lotus, is a symbolic flower in Buddhism. It represents enlightenment, which can come out of suffering just as the beautiful flower grows from slimy mud.

◀ Elephant god

The elephant god Ganesh is the Hindu lord of learning and remover of all obstacles. His parents were Shiva and Parvati. According to Hindu mythology, Shiva mistook his son Ganesh for someone else and beheaded him. Shiva realized his mistake and replaced his son's head with one from the first creature he saw — an elephant.

▲ Gateway to beyond

Many people in Japan practise the Shinto religion. Every Shinto religious shrine can only be entered through a gate called a *torii*. The torii separates the holy shrine from the ordinary world outside. It can be some distance from the shrine itself.

Pathway to Allah ▲

Islamic law schools like this one are found all over the world. Islamic law is known as the *Shari'ah* — an Arabic word meaning a track that leads camels to a waterhole. In the same way, Muslims who obey the Shari'ah will be led to Allah (God).

Stone Age wooden henge

The first stone monuments were built in Europe and date back to around 4200BC. They are called megaliths, from the Greek word meaning 'large stone'. Some of the first megaliths were made up of a large flat stone supported by several upright stones. They are the remains of ancient burial places, called chambered tombs. Others are called passage graves. These were communal graves where many people were buried. Later, larger monuments were constructed. Stone or wood circles called henges, such as Stonehenge in England, were built. No one knows why these circles were made. They may have been temples, meeting places or giant calendars, since they are aligned with the Sun, Moon and stars. The monuments were sometimes altered. Some stones were removed and others were added.

YOU WILL NEED

Card, ruler, pair of compasses, pencil, scissors, self-hardening clay, rolling pin, cutting board, modelling tool, 1cm- and 5mm-thick dowelling, acrylic paint, paintbrush, water pot, fake grass, PVA glue and glue brush, scissors, sandpaper, varnish, brush.

▲ **Stone circle**
The megalithic monuments of Europe have stood for thousands of years, but they have not always looked the same. Archaeologists have found many holes in the ground where additional stones and wooden posts once stood. These sites were once even more complex than they are today.

▸ **The heavy work**
Stonehenge in Wiltshire, England, was built with the simplest technology. The builders probably used sleds or rollers to move the stones, each weighing about 40 tonnes, about 25km to the site. Ropes and levers were then used to haul them into place.

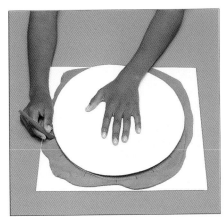

1 Cut out a card circle about 35cm in diameter. Roll out the clay, place the card circle on top and score around the card. Use a modelling tool to mark about 18 points around the circle.

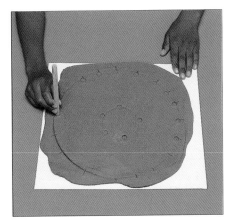

2 Mark another circle, about 10cm across, inside the first circle. Mark five points around it for posts. Press a 1cm-thick stick into each point. Repeat for the outer circle.

3 Make sure all the holes for the posts are evenly spaced. When you have finished, leave the clay base to dry. Then smooth over the base with fine sandpaper and paint it brown.

4 Roughly cover the clay base with pieces of fake grass. Glue them into position as shown above. Be careful not to cover up the holes for the posts you made earlier.

5 Cut seven long and 16 short sticks from the 1cm-thick dowelling. These will make the posts. Cut 17 short pieces from the 5mm-thick dowelling for the lintels. Varnish the sticks.

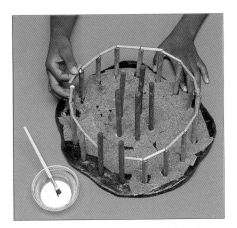

6 When the sticks are dry, glue them in place using the post holes and the picture above as a guide. Then glue the lintels on top of the outer posts to complete your wooden circle.

Wood henges had up to five rings of timber posts increasing in height towards the centre. People started building wooden henges around 3000BC. They became centres of religious and social life.

Egyptian udjat eye

When pharaohs died, everything possible was done to make sure that they completed their journey to the gods in safety. During the New Kingdom, the ruler's coffin, containing his mummy, would be placed on a boat and ferried from Thebes to the west bank of the River Nile. The funeral procession was spectacular. Priests scattered milk and burned incense, and women wept. After the ceremony, the coffin was placed in the tomb with food, drink and charms such as the udjat eye you can make in this project.

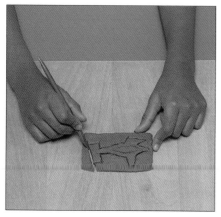

1 Use a rolling pin to roll out some clay on to a cutting board. Use the modelling tool to cut out the pattern of the eye pieces. Refer to step 2 for the shape of each piece.

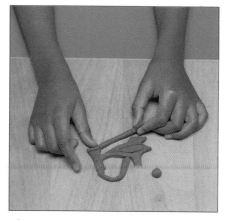

2 Remove the excess clay from the eye pieces and arrange them on the cutting board. The eye is meant to represent the eye of the falcon-headed Egyptian god called Horus.

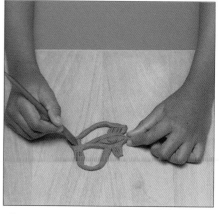

3 Now press the pieces together until you have the full shape of the eye. You may need to use the modelling tool to secure all the joins. When you have finished, leave the eye to dry.

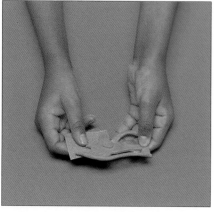

4 When it is dry, smooth the surface of the eye with fine sandpaper. Then wipe it with a soft cloth to remove any dust. The eye of Horus is now ready for painting.

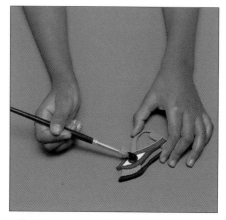

5 Paint in the white of the eye and add the eyebrow and pupil. Next paint in the red liner. Finally, paint the rest of the eye charm blue. Let each colour dry before adding the next.

Horus lost his eye in a battle with Seth, the god of chaos. Udjat eyes were thought to be lucky in ancient Egypt.

Roman temple

Many splendid temples were built to honour the gods and goddesses of the Roman Empire. The Pantheon in Rome was the largest. Special festivals for the gods were held during the year, with processions, music and animal sacrifices. The festivals were often public holidays. The mid-winter celebration of Saturnalia lasted up to seven days. It honoured Saturn, the god of farmers. As the Empire grew, many Romans adopted the religions of other peoples, such as the Egyptians and the Persians.

YOU WILL NEED

Thick card for the template pieces, pencil, ruler, pair of compasses, scissors, newspaper, balloon, PVA glue and glue brush, thin card, masking tape, drinking straws, non-hardening modelling material, acrylic paints, paintbrush, water pot.

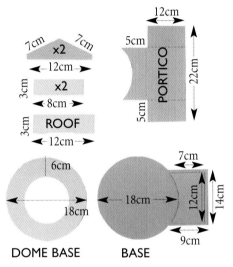

Cut the templates out of thick card, following the measurements above.

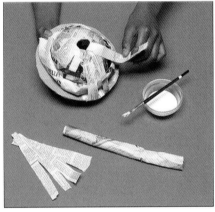

1 Glue layers of paper to half of a balloon. When dry, burst the balloon and cut out a dome. Make a hole in the top. Put the dome on its card base. Bind the pieces together as shown.

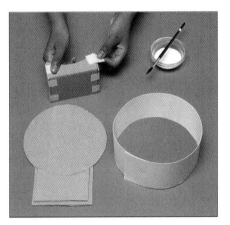

2 Cut a 12cm wide strip of thin card, long enough to fit around the base circle. Secure it with masking tape and then glue it to the base. Tape the portico section together as shown.

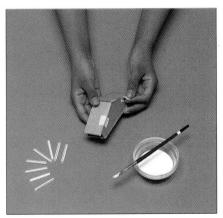

3 Cut some straws into eight pieces, each one 6cm long. These are the columns for the entrance of the temple. Glue and tape together the roof pieces for the entrance to the temple.

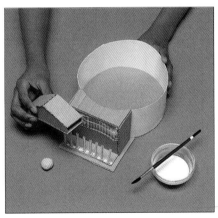

4 Glue everything together as shown and secure with tape. Fix each straw column with a small piece of modelling material at its base. Glue on the roof and the dome. Paint the model.

The Pantheon in Rome was built from AD118 to AD128. It was a temple to all the Roman gods. The Pantheon was built of brick and then clad in stone and marble. Its high dome, mosaic floor, and interior columns remain exactly as they were built.

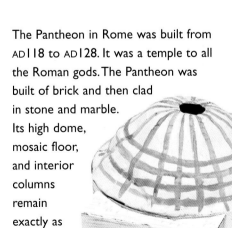

Viking lucky charm

The Vikings believed the universe was held up by a great tree called Yggdrasil. There were several separate worlds. Niflheim was the snowy, cold underworld. The upper world was Asgard, home of the gods.

There were many Viking gods. Odin, the father of the gods, rode through the night sky and his son, Baldr, was god of the summer Sun. Thor, the god of thunder, carried a two-headed hammer. Vikings were superstitious and wore lucky charms, such as one in the shape of Thor's hammer, to protect themselves from evil.

▲ Take it with you

Vikings were buried with the weapons and treasures that they would need for the next life. Even quite poor Vikings were buried with a sword or a brooch.

YOU WILL NEED

Thick paper or card, pencil, scissors, self-hardening clay, cutting board, rolling pin, modelling tool, felt-tipped pen, fine sandpaper, silver acrylic paint, paintbrush, water pot, length of cord, piece of wire.

▲ Pick me, Odin!

Vikings believed that after a battle, Odin and his servants, the Valkyries, searched the battlefield. They carried dead heroes to a Viking heaven called Valholl, or Valhalla.

Draw the outline of Thor's hammer on to thick paper or card using the final project picture as your guide. Cut it out. Use this card hammer as the pattern for making your lucky charm.

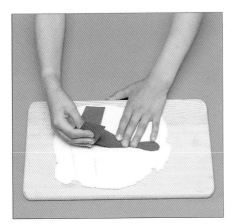

2 Roll out a piece of clay to a thickness of 5mm on the cutting board. Press the card hammer pattern into the clay so that it leaves the outline of the hammer in the clay.

3 Remove the card. Use the modelling tool to cut around the imprint. Mark lines around the edge of the hammer and draw on a pattern. Make a line at the end of the hammer for a handle.

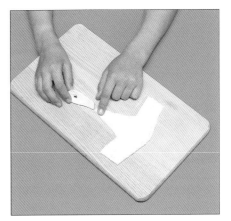

4 Pierce a hole through the end of the handle. Cut off the handle end and turn it upright. Then join the handle back up to the main part of the hammer. Make the join as smooth as possible.

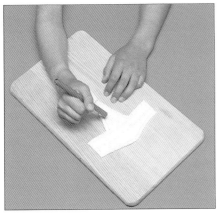

5 Use the end of a felt-tipped pen to make some more impressions on the clay hammer as shown above. When you have finished, leave the clay to dry and completely harden.

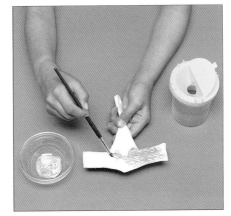

6 When your lucky charm is dry, smooth any rough edges with the sandpaper. Then paint one side silver. Leave it to dry before painting the other side of the lucky charm.

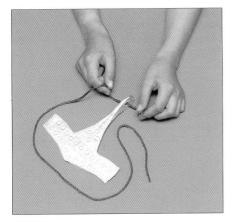

7 When the paint is dry, take a length of cord to fit around your head. Thread the cord through the hole in the hammer. Cut off any excess with the scissors and tie a firm knot.

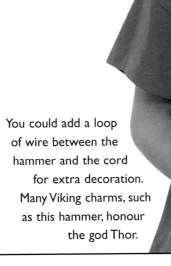

You could add a loop of wire between the hammer and the cord for extra decoration. Many Viking charms, such as this hammer, honour the god Thor.

Tribal dance wand

Dancing was an important part of Native American life. Some of the sacred dances were performed before or after great events such as births, deaths, marriages, hunts or battle, but the occasion was more than just a big party. The Green Corn Dance was held at the Creek New Year and celebrated agricultural growth, and the Arikara Bear Dance aimed to influence the growth of maize and squash crops. Dancers often wore costumes. Cheyenne Sun dancers painted their upper body black (for clouds) with white dots (for hail). Assiniboine Clown dancers often danced and talked backwards and wore masks with long noses.

▲ **Fierce dance**
This is a member of the Huron tribe. He dances in his feathered headdress, brandishing his tomahawk.

▲ **Winter help**
This Woodlands tribe is performing a Snowshoe Dance. Winter was a hard time and food was scarce with few animals around to hunt. The dance asked the spirits for help to survive.

▲ **Mourning dress**
A ghost dance shirt worn by the Sioux during a dance to mourn their dead. European settlers mistakenly saw the dance as provocation to war.

YOU WILL NEED

White paper, pencil, ruler, scissors, acrylic paints, paintbrush, water pot, eight 20cm lengths of 3mm-thick balsa wood, PVA glue and glue brush, pair of compasses, thick card, red and orange paper, 75cm-long stick (1cm thick), string.

I Cut out eight 29cm-long feather shapes from white paper. Make cuts on the top edges, and paint the tips of the feathers black. Glue sticks 12cm from the top of the feathers as shown.

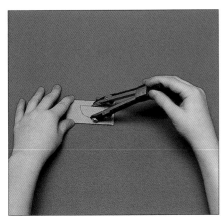

2 Use the compasses and a ruler to measure and draw two semicircles, each with a diameter of 5cm, on to the thick card. Use a pair of scissors to cut out both shapes.

3 Hold the feathers by the sticks. Glue the bottom end of each of the feathers between the two card semicircles. Arrange them around the curved edge of the card as shown.

4 Draw and cut out twelve 6cm-long feather shapes from the red and orange paper. Make another eight red feathers, each 2.5cm long. Make feathery cuts along the top edges.

5 Divide the 6cm-long feathers in two, and glue them to each end of the 75cm-long stick. Secure them with a piece of string tied around the bottom of the feathers as shown.

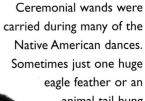

6 Paint the semicircles cream and then leave them to dry. Bend back the two straight edges. Place the flaps either side of the centre of the stick. Glue the flaps firmly in place.

Ceremonial wands were carried during many of the Native American dances. Sometimes just one huge eagle feather or an animal tail hung from the top.

7 Glue the 2.5cm-long red feathers to the outside tips of each black feather. Leave the dance wand to dry completely. Your wand will then be ready, so let the dance begin.

Chancay doll

Archaeologists have found many burial sites in the Andes Mountains. As early as 3200BC, Andean peoples had learned how to mummify (preserve) bodies. Respect for ancestors was an important part of the civilizations in the Andes. The Chancays were an ancient people who lived on the coast of central Peru. They were conquered by the mighty Incas in the 1500s. Dolls such as the one you can make in this project were placed in the graves of the Chancays to help them in the afterlife.

Final resting place ▶

The body of an Inca noble wrapped in cloth is carried to a *chulpa* (tomb). Chulpas were tall stone towers used to bury important people in ancient Peru.

YOU WILL NEED

Cream calico fabric, pencil, ruler, scissors, acrylic paints, paintbrush, water pot, black wool, PVA glue and glue brush, wadding, 20 red pipe cleaners, red wool.

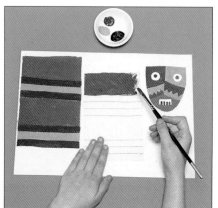

1 Draw two rectangles 16 x 11cm on cream calico fabric to make the doll's body. Then draw two shield shapes 7 x 8cm for the head. Paint the body and one head as shown. Cut them out.

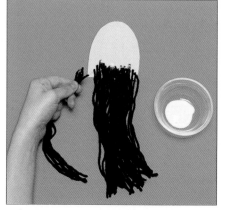

2 Cut 35 strands of black wool, each measuring 18cm in length. These will make the doll's hair. Glue each wool strand evenly along the top of the unpainted head shape as shown.

3 Cut a piece of wadding slightly smaller than the head shape. Glue the wadding on top of the hair and the head piece below. Then glue the painted face on top as shown. Leave to dry.

4 For each arm, take five pipe cleaners and cut each one 11cm long. Twist the pipe cleaners together to within 1.5cm of one end. Splay the open end to make the doll's fingers.

5 Make the legs for the doll in the same way, but this time twist all the way down and bend the ends to make feet. Wind red wool around the doll's arms and legs to hide the twists.

6 Assemble the pieces of the doll using the picture above as your guide, using glue to fix wadding between the pieces. Then glue the front piece of the doll's body in place as shown.

7 Glue the head to the front of the doll's body, making sure the hair does not become caught in the join. Leave the doll to dry completely before picking it up.

▲ Inca mask

This face mask is made of beaten gold and dates back to the 1100s or 1200s. It was made by a Chimú goldsmith and was laid in a royal grave.

Dolls such as these were placed in the graves of the Chancay people of the central Peruvian coast. The Chancay believed that grave dolls such as these would serve as helpers in the life to come.

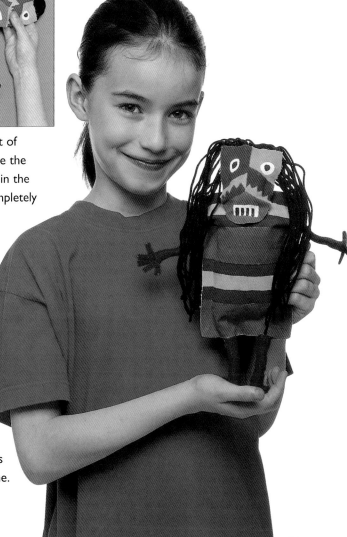

Theatre and Entertainment

▲ Poets' corner

Poets such as Tao Yuanmin were highly respected in ancient China. Poetry dates back over 3,000 years in China. It was sung rather than spoken.

Throughout history, people from every country and culture have enjoyed listening to music, reading stories and poetry and watching dance, drama and shows. Artistic styles vary in different parts of the world, but representing important events and rituals in human society has always been a big part of our lives.

Many arts aim to entertain their audience by bringing an event or story vividly to life. The arts are also an excellent way of introducing people to new ideas. They are sometimes used to influence their audience's thoughts and beliefs.

◀ Festive times

Festivals were an important part of Inca society. This one is Situa, which was held in August to ward off illness. Music and dance played a large role during these occasions. People would play musical instruments such as drums, whistles and rattles all day.

An actor's disguise ▶

The ancient Greeks enjoyed music and art and went to the theatre regularly. The actors wore special masks during a performance. The top mask was used in tragedies, the one at the bottom in comedies.

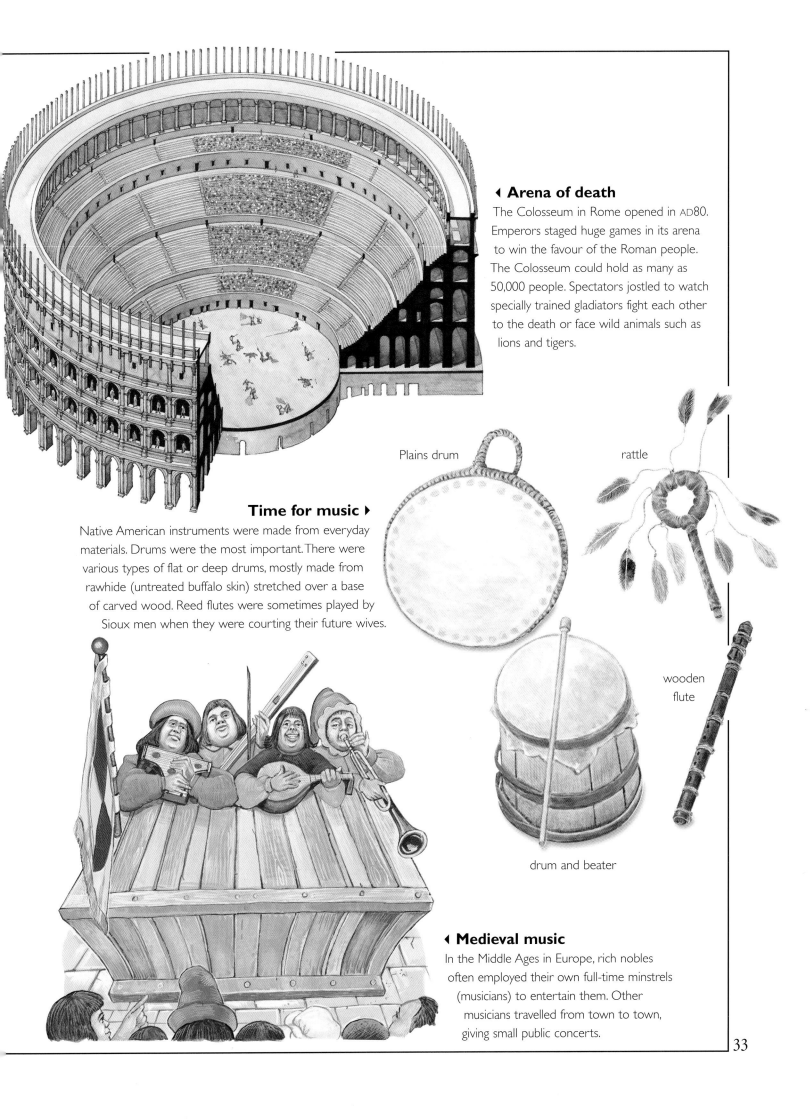

◀ Arena of death

The Colosseum in Rome opened in AD80.
Emperors staged huge games in its arena
to win the favour of the Roman people.
The Colosseum could hold as many as
50,000 people. Spectators jostled to watch
specially trained gladiators fight each other
to the death or face wild animals such as
lions and tigers.

Plains drum

rattle

Time for music ▶

Native American instruments were made from everyday
materials. Drums were the most important. There were
various types of flat or deep drums, mostly made from
rawhide (untreated buffalo skin) stretched over a base
of carved wood. Reed flutes were sometimes played by
Sioux men when they were courting their future wives.

wooden
flute

drum and beater

◀ Medieval music

In the Middle Ages in Europe, rich nobles
often employed their own full-time minstrels
(musicians) to entertain them. Other
musicians travelled from town to town,
giving small public concerts.

33

Greek Medusa's costume

In ancient Greek mythology, the Gorgons were three sisters called Stheno, Euryale and Medusa. They were the daughters of two sea monsters and had writhing, living snakes instead of hair, tusks like boars, gold wings and hands of bronze. Two of the Gorgons were immortal but the youngest sister, Medusa, was killed by the Greek hero Perseus. He cut off her head and gave it as a present to his guardian goddess Athene. She wore it ever after like a monstrous brooch on the front of her cloak.

YOU WILL NEED

2 x 2m green fabric, soft-leaded pencil, ruler, scissors, PVA glue and glue brush, sheet of thick card, pair of compasses, dark green acrylic paint, paintbrush, water pot, pair of green tights, 40 pipe cleaners, red card, needle and thread.

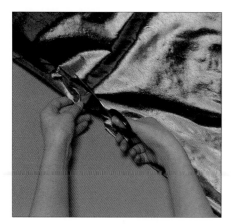

1 Fold the green fabric square in half. Along the centre of the fold, mark a narrow crescent shape 20cm long using a soft-leaded pencil. Cut out the crescent of fabric.

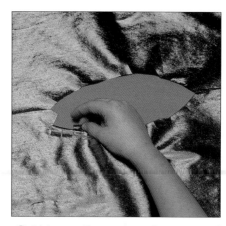

2 Make small cuts along the centre of the hole to create a series of flaps. Fold each flap over and glue it down as shown above. This gives the neck hole a neat, even edge.

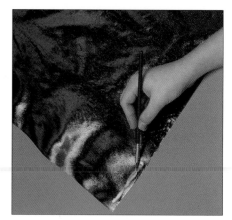

3 Fold over and glue down any frayed edges of fabric to complete your gown. Leave it to one side to dry completely while you make the rest of the Medusa's costume.

4 Use the compasses and ruler to measure and draw a circle with a radius of 7cm (diameter 14cm) on to the sheet of thick card as shown. Carefully cut out the card circle.

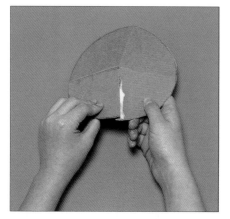

5 Cut into the centre of the circle. Bend the card slightly, overlapping the two edges, and glue them into position as shown above. Leave to dry, then paint the card dark green.

6 Cut the foot and an extra 20cm of the leg from a pair of green tights. Stretch the foot over the card circle so that it lies over the centre of the card as shown above.

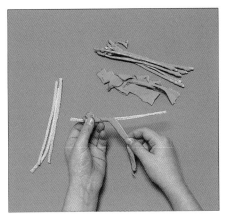

7 Cut the remainder of the tights fabric into small strips and wrap them around 40 pipe cleaners as shown above. Dab a spot of glue on each end to secure the strips in place.

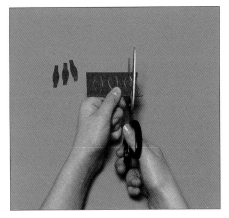

8 Draw small snake head shapes on the red card. Make 40 heads about 2.5cm long and 1cm wide at the ends. Cut them out. (You could fold the card over and cut out two at a time.)

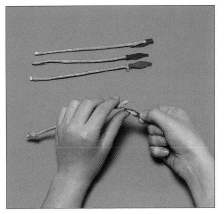

9 Glue the snake heads on to the ends of the pipe cleaners. Leave the snakes to one side until the glue is completely dry. You are now ready to fit the snakes to the headpiece.

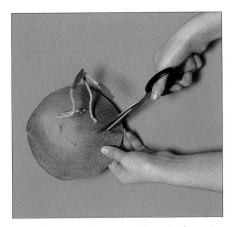

10 Using the pointed end of a pair of scissors, carefully pierce 20 small holes through the headpiece you made earlier. Take care to space the holes out evenly.

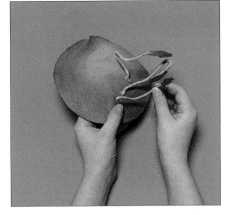

11 Poke a pipe cleaner through each hole. Bend the ends on the inside of the headpiece to hold them in position. Form the pipe cleaners into twisted snake shapes.

12 Curve the unused pipe cleaners into twisty snake shapes. Use a needle and thread to sew them over the excess tights fabric that hangs around the card headpiece as shown.

To complete the gown, tie a green cord around your waist. If you have any extra fabric, make a scarf for your neck. Paint your face green to add to the scary effect. The only way to see a Gorgon without being turned to stone was to look at their reflection on a shiny surface. Clever Perseus, who defeated Medusa, used his shield.

Chinese mask

The earliest Chinese poetry was sung rather than spoken. *Shijing* (the 'Book of Songs') dates back over 3,000 years and includes the words to hymns and folk songs. Music was an important part of Chinese life, and models of musicians were often put in tombs to provide entertainment in the afterlife.

Musicians were frequently accompanied by acrobats, jugglers and magicians. Such acts were as popular in the markets and streets of the town as in the courtyards of nobles. Storytelling and puppet shows were equally well loved. Plays and opera became popular in the 1200s, with tales of murder, intrigue, heroism and love acted out to music. Most of the female roles would be played by men. Elaborate make-up and fancy costumes made it clear to the audience whether the actor was playing a hero or a villain, a princess or a demon.

▲ New Year dragon

Dressing up is also a popular part of Chinese religion, with everybody joining in events such as Chinese New Year. Dragons symbolize happiness and good luck and represent the generous spirit of New Year.

YOU WILL NEED

Tape measure, self-hardening clay, cutting board, modelling tool, petroleum jelly, newspaper, PVA glue and glue brush, water, bowl for mixing glue and water, thick card, pencil, ruler, scissors, masking tape, two large white beads, acrylic paints, paintbrush, water pot, wood glue, needle, black wool, string.

▲ Energetic opera

Some ancient Chinese plays are still performed today. Modern theatre companies try to recreate how plays would have looked to their original audience.

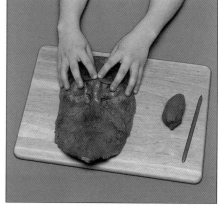

Measure the dimensions of your face using a ruler or tape measure. Mould a piece of clay to fit the size of your face. Carve out eye sockets and attach a clay nose. Leave to dry.

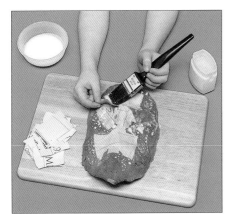

2 Smear the front of the mask with petroleum jelly. Apply six layers of papier mâché, made by soaking strips of newspaper in two parts PVA glue to one part water. Leave the mask to dry.

3 When it is dry, remove the mask from the clay mould. Cut a 2.5cm-wide strip of card long enough to fit around your face. Bend it into a circle. Tape it to the back of the mask.

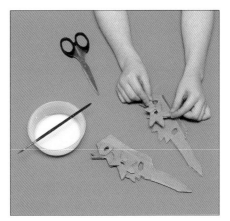

4 Cut two pointed ear shapes as shown. Fold the card at the straight edges to make flaps. Cut out and glue on decorative pieces of card. Glue the ear flaps to the sides of the mask.

5 Glue two large white beads on to the front of the mask for the eyes. Cut out more small pieces of card. Glue these on for eyebrows. Glue on another piece of card for the lips.

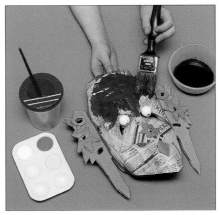

6 Paint the entire mask in a dark blue-grey. Leave it to dry. Paint on more details using brighter colours. When the mask is dry, varnish it with wood glue.

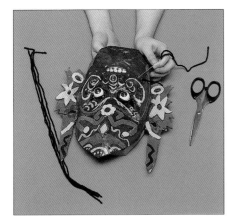

7 Use a needle to thread lengths of black wool through for the beard. Tape the wool at the back. Then thread string through the sides of the mask behind the ears to tie it on.

Highly decorative masks such as this one were worn to great effect in the Chinese opera. Folk tales were acted out to the dramatic sound of crashing cymbals and high-pitched singing.

Japanese Noh mask

Going to the theatre and listening to music were popular pastimes in ancient Japan. There were several kinds of Japanese drama, all of which developed from religious dances at temples and shrines, or from slow, stately dances performed at the emperor's court.

Noh is the oldest form of Japanese drama. It developed in the 1300s from rituals and dances that had been performed for centuries before. Noh plays were serious and dignified. The actors performed on a bare stage, with only a backdrop. They chanted or sang their words, and the performance was accompanied by percussion and a flute. Noh performances were traditionally held in the open air, often at a shrine. Kabuki plays were first seen around 1600 and were a complete contrast to the tragic Noh style. In 1629, the shoguns (military governors) banned women performers and so male actors took their places. Kabuki plays became very popular in the new, fast-growing towns.

▲ Wooden expression
This Noh mask represents a warrior. Noh drama did not try to be lifelike. The actors moved very slowly using stylized gestures to show their feelings.

YOU WILL NEED

Tape measure, balloon, petroleum jelly, mixing bowl, newspaper, PVA glue, water, pin, scissors, felt-tipped pen, self-hardening clay, bradawl, acrylic paints, paintbrush, water pot, piece of cord.

◄ Plays made fun
Kabuki plays were very different to the more serious Noh style theatre. They were fast-moving, loud, flashy and very dramatic. Audiences admired the skills of the Kabuki actors as much as the cleverness or thoughtfulness of the plots of these plays.

I Ask a friend to measure around your head, above the ears, with a tape measure. Blow up a balloon to the same size. This will act as the mould for the papier mâché mask.

2 Smear the balloon with a layer of petroleum jelly. Then rip up strips of old newspaper and soak them in a bowl containing a mixture of two parts PVA glue to one parts water.

3 Cover the front and sides of the balloon with the papier mâché. You will need to add three or four layers of papier mâché. When the mask is dry, pop the balloon.

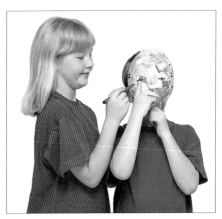

4 Trim the papier mâché to tidy up the edges of your mask. Then ask a friend to mark where your eyes and mouth are when you hold the mask to your face.

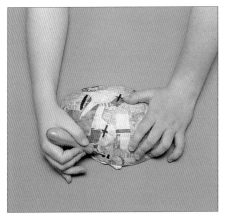

5 Cut out holes for the eyes and mouth using scissors. Then put a piece of clay either side of the face at eye level. Use a bradawl to pierce two holes on each side of the face.

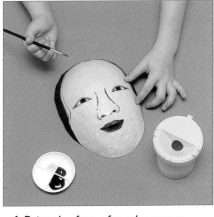

6 Paint the face of a calm young lady from Noh theatre on to your mask. You can use the picture above as your guide. In Japan, this mask would have been worn by a man.

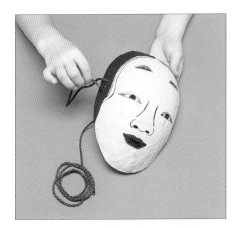

7 Fit a length of cord through the holes at each side of the mask. Tie one end of the cord. Once you have adjusted the mask to fit your head, firmly tie the other end of the cord.

Put on your mask and feel like an actor in an ancient Noh play. Noh drama was always about important and serious topics. Favourite subjects included death and the afterlife, and the plays were often tragic.

Celtic harp

The Celts enjoyed music, poems and songs as entertainment and for more serious purposes, too. Music was played to accompany Celtic warriors into battle and help them feel brave. Poems praised the achievements of a great chieftain or the adventures of bold raiders, and recorded the history of a tribe. Dead chieftains and heroes, and possibly even ordinary people, were mourned with sad laments.

On special occasions, and in the homes of high-ranking Celts, poems and songs were performed by people called bards. Roman writers described the many years of training to become a bard. Bards learned how to compose using all the different styles of poetry and memorized hundreds of legends and songs. They also learned how to play an instrument, and to read and write. Becoming a bard was the first step towards being a druid (priest).

▲ Making music
Instruments such as this stringed lute have been played by humans as far back as 3500BC – long before the age of the Celtic civilization.

YOU WILL NEED

Sheet of thin card (49 x 39cm), pencil, ruler, scissors, thick card (49 x 39cm), felt-tipped pen, PVA glue and glue brush, acrylic paint, paintbrush, water pot, bradawl, coloured string, 16 brass split pins.

◀ Music from a god
This statue shows a Celtic god playing a lyre. Music played an important part in many Celtic ceremonies. The Celts believed that, like religious knowledge, music was too holy to be written down. Sadly, this means that many Celtic poems and songs have been lost forever.

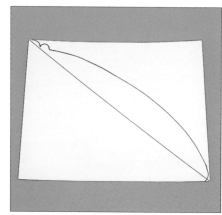

Draw a diagonal line, from corner to corner, on the rectangle of thin card. Then draw a gently curving line, with a shape at one end, using the picture above as your guide.

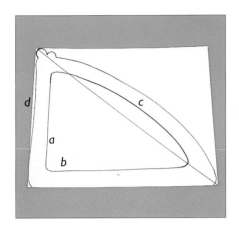

2 Using the picture above as your guide, draw two lines – *a* and *b* – 4.5cm in from the edge of the card. Join them with a curved line *c*. Finally, add a curved line *d* parallel with *a*.

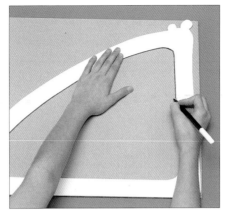

3 Cut out the harp shape you have drawn and place it on the rectangle of thick card. Draw around it, inside and out, with a felt-tipped pen. Cut out the harp shape from the thick card.

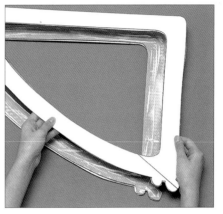

4 Glue one side of the thin card harp shape to one side of the thick card harp shape. Apply two coats of dark brown paint, leaving the harp shape to dry between each coat.

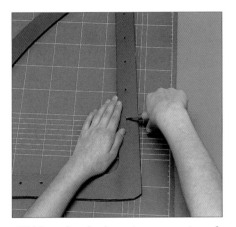

5 Use a bradawl to pierce a series of seven holes approximately 5cm apart along the two straight sides of the frame of your harp. These will be the holes for the strings.

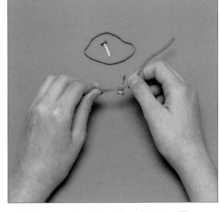

6 Cut a 40cm length of string. Then cut six more pieces of string, each one 5cm shorter than the last. Tie a brass split pin to both ends of all the pieces of string.

Most Celtic poetry was not spoken, but sung or chanted to the music of the harp or lyre. Bards used the music to create the right atmosphere to accompany their words, and to add extra dramatic affects, such as shivery sounds during a scary ghost tale.

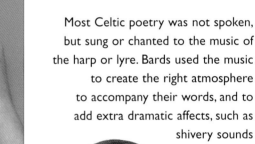

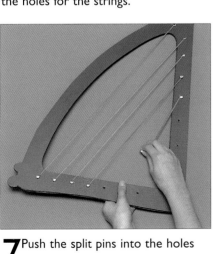

7 Push the split pins into the holes you made earlier so that the strings lie diagonally across the harp. Adjust each string so that it is stretched tightly across the frame.

Inca hand drum

Music and dance were very important to the Incas. Instruments, such as rattles, flutes, large drums, hand drums and panpipes, were made from wood, reeds, pottery and bone. At festivals, such as the Inti Raymi (Sun Festival), musicians would play all day without a break. Large bands walked in procession, each panpipe player picking out a different part of the tune. The Spanish influenced these festivals after the conquest, and they became known by the Spanish term, *fiesta*. However, many of the fiestas celebrated had their dances or costumes rooted in an Inca past.

▲ **Traditional music**
A modern street band plays in Cuzco, the ancient capital of the Inca Empire. Ancient tunes and rhythms live on in the modern music of the Andes.

▲ **Home of the Incas**
The Inca Empire in the Peruvian Andes was a world full of music and dance, especially during festivals.

YOU WILL NEED

Pencil, ruler, thick card (100 x 20cm), scissors, masking tape, cream calico fabric, PVA glue and glue brush, acrylic paints, paintbrush, water pot, wadding, 30cm length of thick dowelling, coloured wool.

I Use a pencil and ruler to mark two rectangles on the thick card, each one measuring 85 x 9cm. Cut the rectangles out carefully. They will form the sides of your Inca hand drum.

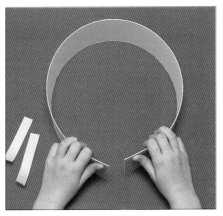

2 Bend one rectangle into a circle as shown above. Use strips of masking tape to join the two ends of the card ring together. It may be easier to ask a friend to help you do this.

3 Lay the ring on top of the cream calico fabric. Draw around the card ring on to the fabric, leaving a gap of about 2cm as shown above. Remove the ring and cut out the fabric circle.

4 Paint glue around the edge of the fabric circle. Turn the fabric over. Carefully stretch the fabric over the card ring. Keep the fabric taut and smooth the edges as you stick.

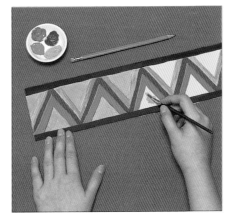

5 Draw a geometric Inca-style pattern on the second strip of card. Use bright colours to decorate the card as shown above. Lay the card flat and leave it to dry.

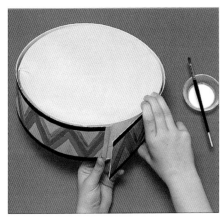

6 When the painted strip is dry, wrap it around the drum as shown. Use masking tape to fix one end of the ring to the drum. Then glue the rest of the ring around the drum. Leave to dry.

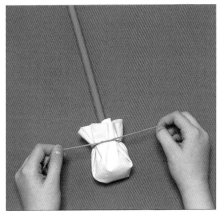

7 Cut out a 20cm-diameter circle of calico fabric. Make a drumstick by wrapping a piece of wadding and the calico circle around one end of the dowelling. Tie it with wool.

Women played hand drums like this one at festivals during Inca times. Some festivals were held in villages and fields. Others took place at religious sites or in the big Inca cities.

Playing the fool

Noble families often employed jesters full-time, so that they could be cheered up whenever they wanted. It was rather like having their own private comedy act. Jesters dressed in silly costumes with bells and played the fool. However, they were often skilled jugglers and acrobats, too. They sang songs and told funny stories and jokes, which were often very rude. They often made fun of their audience, and were great at passing on top-secret gossip that no one else would dare mention.

▲ Roll up for the fair
In the Middle Ages, jesters were often found entertaining merchants and traders at the local markets and fairs.

Juggling

YOU WILL NEED

Juggling: juggling balls.

Jester's rattle: pencil, yellow card (24 x 19cm), polystyrene ball, scissors, PVA glue and glue brush, 40cm length of dowelling (1cm in diameter), acrylic paints, paintbrush, water pot, seven bells, two 45cm lengths each of red and yellow ribbon.

1 Take a juggling ball in each hand. Throw both of the balls up into the air together in straight lines and catch them when they fall. This is the easy part of juggling!

2 Throw both juggling balls up together so that they cross in front of you. The trick is to make sure that they do not bump into each other. Catch each ball in the opposite hand.

3 Now try throwing both balls up together in straight lines again. This time, however, cross your hands over to catch the balls as they fall. You may have to practise this one a lot!

4 Throw the juggling ball in your right hand diagonally across your body. Just as it is about to drop, throw the other ball diagonally towards your right hand. Keep practising!

5 Catch the first ball in your left hand but keep your eye on the other ball still in the air. Catch this one in your right hand. Remember – practise makes perfect!

Jester's rattle

1 Use a pencil to draw a hat shape on to the piece of yellow card. Use the picture above to help you. Draw around the ball to make sure the curve at the bottom is the same diameter.

2 Cut out the hat shape. Put a strip of glue around the curve at the bottom of the hat. Press the ball into the glued section and hold it in place until it is firmly stuck down.

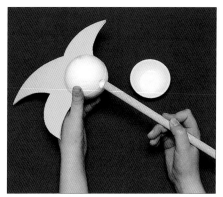

3 Use the pointed ends of a pair of scissors to make a hole in the bottom of the ball. Ask an adult to help if necessary. Fill the hole with glue and insert the piece of dowelling.

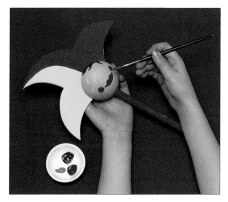

4 Paint the stick bright red. When it is dry, paint some eyes, a mouth, cheeks and hair on the ball to make a cheerful face. Then paint one half of the jester's hat red.

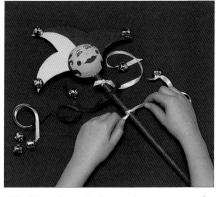

5 Glue three bells to the corners of the hat. Then tie four bells to the lengths of coloured ribbon. Tie the ribbons around the stick, using a simple knot to secure them.

Once you know how to juggle two balls, try to master the three-ball juggle. Professional jugglers who were not employed full-time travelled from castle to castle.

Important people often carried sticks in the Middle Ages, which they banged loudly on the floor to attract attention. The jester's small stick made fun of these.

Monster mask

Myths and legends involving beasts, ghouls and witches have captured the imaginations of people worldwide. Such scary stories have passed through the generations, at first by word of mouth, and then through books, plays, films and now via the Internet. The tale of Frankenstein's monster, created by the English writer Mary Shelley, is one such spine-chilling story. The monster was an ugly creature brought to life by a young scientist called Frankenstein. In this project, you can make a mask of Frankenstein's monster.

YOU WILL NEED

Balloon, newspaper strips, water, PVA glue and glue brush, pin, scissors, thick card (29 x 14cm, 22 x 12cm, 29 x 9.5cm and scraps), ruler, pencil, pair of compasses, brown gum tape, masking tape, two 3cm lengths of thin balsa dowelling, acrylic paints, paintbrushes, water pot, string.

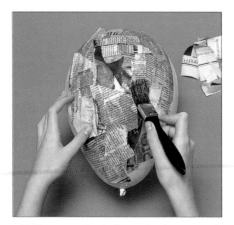

1 Blow up the balloon. Soak strips of newspaper with half measures of glue and water to make papier mâché. Cover one side of the balloon with five layers of papier mâché. Leave it to dry.

2 When the mask is completely dry, carefully burst the balloon using a pin. Take the papier mâché mask and trim off the excess to produce a rounded face shape.

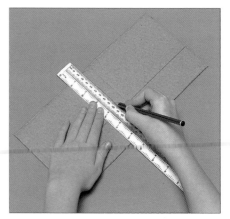

3 Take the piece of card measuring 29 x 14cm. Use a ruler and pencil to draw a line 5cm in from one long edge. Then draw a pencil line across the middle as shown above.

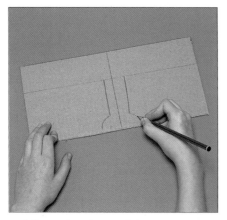

4 Draw the shape of the nose using the centre line in the middle as a guide. Make the nose 3cm wide on the bridge and 4cm at the nostril. Cut out the nose and the brow.

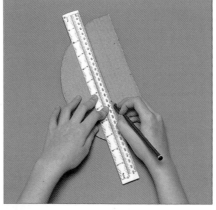

5 Set the compasses to 11cm. Draw a semicircle on to the 22 x 12cm piece of card. Cut it out. Draw a pencil line 5cm from the straight edge. Cut this 5cm piece off.

6 Line the edges of the semicircle with PVA glue. Stick it to the top edge of the nose piece as shown above. Hold the pieces together until the glue has dried.

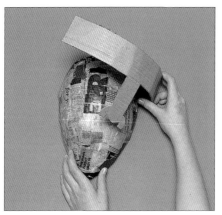

7 Cover the back of the head and nose piece with PVA glue. Stick this piece in position on top of the papier mâché face mask you made earlier. Leave the mask to one side to dry.

8 Draw a line in the centre of the 29 x 9.5cm piece of card. Draw a 10 x 4cm rectangle at the centre of the line touching the bottom edge. Cut the smaller rectangle out.

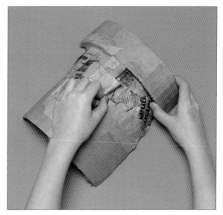

9 Cover the back of the card jaw piece with glue. Stick it over the lower part of the mask. Cover the gaps between the stuck-on face parts and the mask with brown gum tape.

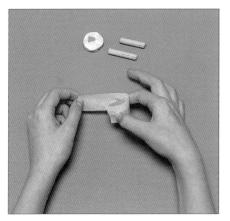

10 Set the compasses to 1cm and draw two circles on a scrap piece of card. Cut out the two circles and cover them with masking tape. Take the balsa dowelling.

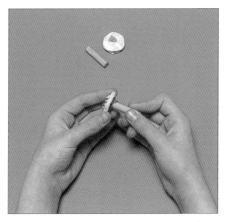

11 Make a hole in the centre of each card circle using your scissors. Push the balsa dowelling through the middle. Glue into position and paint the pieces black.

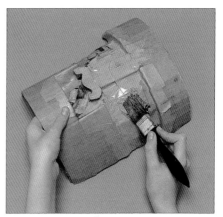

12 Paint the mask with a base colour, for example, grey or green. Wait for the base coat to dry before painting in the details of the face with other colours. Leave to dry.

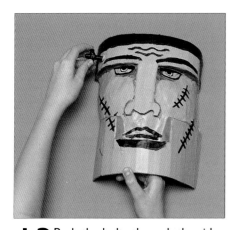

13 Push the bolts through the sides of the mask. Glue them into position. Put the mask over your face and mark eyeholes. Take the mask off. Make eyeholes with the scissors.

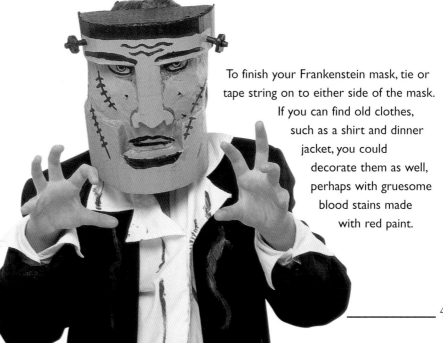

To finish your Frankenstein mask, tie or tape string on to either side of the mask. If you can find old clothes, such as a shirt and dinner jacket, you could decorate them as well, perhaps with gruesome blood stains made with red paint.

Toys and Games

▲ Game players

Archaeologists have found board games and toys among the remains of the great cities of the Indus Valley civilization. These people grew up nearly 5,000 years ago in the area occupied by present-day Pakistan.

Peeople have always played with toys and games. Our early Stone Age ancestors played with small doll-like figures made of clay and whistles carved from bone. Toys dating from 5000BC have been found in China. Many games from the ancient world are still familiar to us today. Hopscotch and hide-and-seek were played in the ancient civilizations of Egypt, Greece and Rome. There were toys, too, such as rattles, yo-yos, dolls and spinning tops.

As well as being fun, games provided mental and physical challenges. Board games in particular showed children different ways of thinking and planning, and prepared them for the adult world.

◀ Martial arts

Kendo and several other martial arts that are popular today developed from the fighting skills of samurai warriors from ancient Japan. In kendo, combatants fight one another with long swords made of split bamboo. They score points by managing to touch their opponent's body, not by cutting or stabbing them.

Royal game ▶

A beautifully made board game was found in the Royal Graves of Ur, an ancient city of Mesopotamia. The board game was made of wood covered in bitumen (tar) and decorated with a mosaic of shell, bone, blue lapis lazuli (a kind of gemstone), red glass and pink limestone. The game may have been a bit like ludo, with two sets of counters and four-sided dice, but the rules have not been found.

◀ Ancient athletes

Sport was important to the ancient Greeks. In fact, it had religious significance. The first ever Olympic Games were held in 776BC in honour of the Greek god Zeus. Sports included throwing the discus and javelin, boxing, wrestling and the long jump. The games were only open to men – women were not even allowed to watch. They held their own games in honour of Hera, goddess of women.

Dangerous sports ▶

Wrestling was a favourite sport as long ago as 1000BC. Many kings in ancient India had the title *malla* (wrestler). They had to keep to strict diets and physical training programmes in camps known as *akharas*. Wrestling could be a highly dangerous activity. One inscription tells of a malla who was accidentally killed during a match.

Egyptian snake game

Board games such as mehen, or the snake game, were popular from the earliest days of ancient Egypt. In the tomb of the Pharaoh Tutankhamun, a beautiful gaming board made of ebony and ivory was discovered. It was designed for a board game called senet. Players threw sticks to decide how many squares to move at a time. Some of the squares had gains and some had forfeits. Senet was thought to symbolize the struggle against evil.

Another favourite pastime for the ancient Egyptians was sport. Armed with bows and arrows, sticks, spears and nets, they hunted wild animals for pleasure as well as for food. Wrestling was a popular spectator sport at all levels of society. Chariot racing, however, which was introduced around 1663BC, could only be afforded by the nobility.

▲ Tomb raider

A thief breaks into a pharaoh's tomb. Inside are the treasures that were important to him, including game boards and counters.

YOU WILL NEED

Self-hardening clay, rolling pin, cutting board, ruler, modelling tool, acrylic paint, paintbrush, water pot, cloth, varnish, 12 counters (six blue and grey and six gold and orange), two large counters, dice, pencil.

▲ Games in the afterlife

The walls of many Egyptian tombs were covered with everyday scenes. They were designed to show how life should carry on in the afterlife. In this tomb painting, an official of the Pharaoh Rameses II is playing the board game of senet with his wife.

Roll out the clay on to a board and cut it into the shape shown above. Score on a snake shape and score lines across the body at intervals. Use the final project picture as a guide.

2 When the clay is completely dry, rub the board with diluted green paint to stain the lines. Wipe away the excess paint with a cloth. Leave the board to dry and then varnish it.

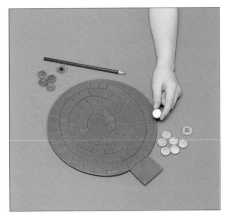

3 Each player takes six counters of the same colours, plus one large piece called a 'lion'. Place the counters so that the same colour faces up. Throw the dice. You need a '1' to start each counter.

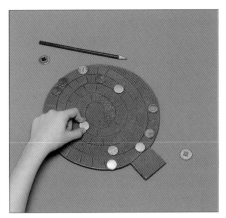

4 Your go ends if you throw another '1'. If it's another number, advance a counter that number of squares towards the centre of the board. Only move counters that have started on the board.

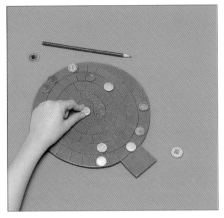

5 Throw exactly the right number to reach the centre. Then turn the counter over so that it can start the return journey. As soon as your first counter gets home, the lion piece begins.

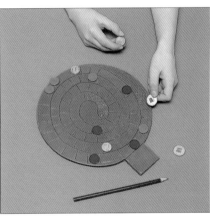

6 The lion counter moves to the centre of the board in the same way as the other counters. On its return journey, it can eat the opponent's counters if it lands on them.

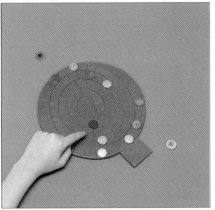

7 The winner is the person whose lion has eaten the largest number of counters. Work out the number of counters you got home safely, and see who has the most counters left.

▲ Two in one

This board game set, found in a pharaoh's pyramid, could be used to play senet and another game called tjau. It has a built-in drawer that contained all the loose pieces, such as counters, for the two games.

Mehen, the snake game, was popular in Egypt before 3000BC. The game was called snake because the stone board represented a coiled serpent with its head in the middle.

Greek knucklebones

The game of knucklebones played in ancient Greece is rather like the more modern game of jacks. It was not a game at all to begin with. The way the bones fell when they were thrown was interpreted to predict the future. The knuckles – little anklebones of a sheep or cow – were called *astragalos* by the Greeks. Girls tended to play the game of knucklebones, while boys preferred to cast the bones like dice in a game of chance. Each of the four distinctively shaped sides of the bone was given a different numerical value.

One of the most popular board games in ancient Greece was a game of siege called *polis* (city). Another was the 'game of the five lines', in which the central, sacred, line had special significance. The exact rules are not known, but it is thought that it may have been rather like the later game of draughts. Board and picture games, and toys have been found in the tombs of children. Many archaeological finds have unearthed evidence of toys that are still played with today, such as hoops, rattles, dolls, spinning tops and balls.

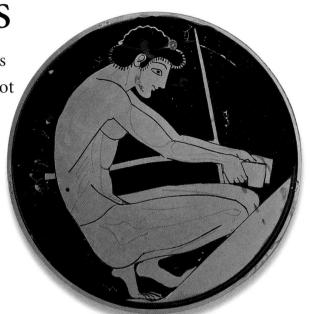

▲ Fit for life
A Greek athlete lifts weights, perhaps to get himself fit for battle, or for a sports competition. The Greeks were keen on sport for its own sake. Many cities had a public gymnasium, and games were a feature of religious festivals.

> ## YOU WILL NEED
> Self-hardening clay, rolling pin, cutting board, modelling tool, cream acrylic paint, paintbrush, water pot.

▲ Knockout punch
Boxing was one of the sports soon included in the Olympic Games after they began in 776BC. Other sports included weights, discus and javelin, running and wrestling.

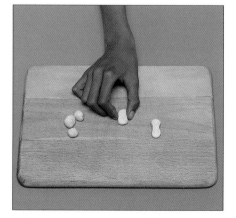

I Divide the clay into five small pieces. Then roll each piece into the shape of a ball. Press each ball of clay into a figure-of-eight shape as shown in the picture above.

2 Use the modelling tool to carve out a ridge in the middle of each figure-of-eight. Then make small dents in the end of each piece with your finger. Leave the five shapes to dry.

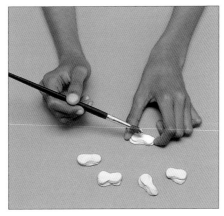

3 When they are dry, give the pieces two coats of paint. Use cream paint so that the pieces look like bone. When the paint is dry, you and a friend can play with them.

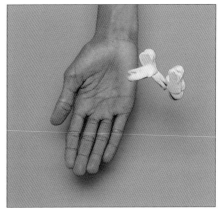

4 To play knucklebones, gather the five pieces in the palm of one of your hands. Throw all five pieces into the air at once as shown above. Then quickly flip your hand over.

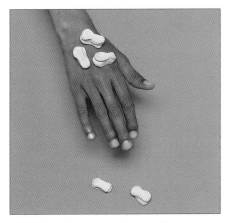

5 Take turns to try to catch as many of the pieces as you can on the back of your hand. If you or your friend catch them all that person wins the game. If not, the game continues.

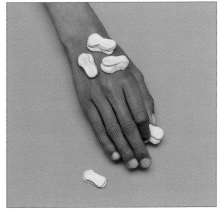

6 If you drop any of the pieces, try to pick them up with the others still on the back of your hand. Throw them with your free hand and try to catch them again.

Knucklebones were made from the anklebones of animals such as sheep or cows. These small bones were used in different ways, depending on the type of game. The Greeks also used the knucklebones as dice.

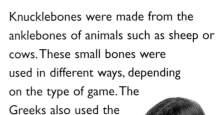

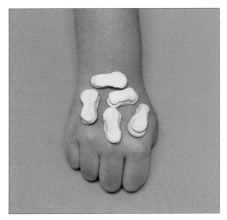

7 The winner is the first person to catch all the knucklebones on the back of their hand. It may take a few goes to get the hang of the game. But remember – practice makes perfect!

53

Roman dux game

The Roman game of dux was a little bit like the game of draughts. In terms of difficulty, it comes somewhere between the very simple games that Romans enjoyed playing, such as noughts and crosses, and more complicated games, such as chess. In some games, a die was thrown to decide how many squares they could move at a time.

Knucklebones was popular at public baths. The Romans learned how to play the game from the Greeks. Each player would throw the small anklebones of a sheep up into the air and try to catch them on the back of the hand. Knucklebones could also be played like dice, with each side of the bones having a different score.

Roman children played games such as hide-and-seek and hopscotch, and had dolls and toy animals of wood, clay or bronze. A child from a wealthy family might be given a child-sized chariot that could be pulled by a goat.

▲ **Playing games**
The mosaic dates from around the 1st century AD. It shows three Roman men playing a dice game. The Romans were such great gamblers that games of chance were officially banned. The one exception was during the winter festival of Saturnalia, when most rules were relaxed.

▲ **Counter culture**
Plain, round gaming counters like these were made of bone or ivory. The Romans sometimes used counters that had been carved into the shape of animals' heads or decorated with a picture in relief (raised from the surface).

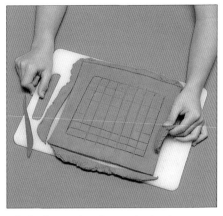

1 Roll out the clay, and trim it to about 25cm square. Use the ruler and modelling tool to mark out a grid eight squares across and eight squares down. Leave room for a border.

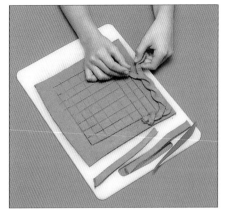

2 Decorate the border using the excess clay as shown. Leave the gaming board to dry. Each player then chooses a colour and has 16 tiles and a bead. The bead is the dux, or leader.

3 Players take turns to put their tiles on the squares, two at a time. The dux is put on last. Players now take turns to move a tile one square forward, backwards or sideways.

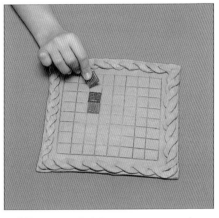

4 If you sandwich your opponent's tile between two of your own, his or her tile is captured and removed. You then get an extra go. The dux is captured in the same way as the tiles.

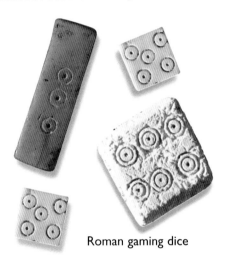

Roman gaming dice

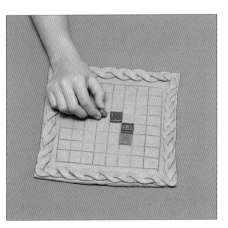

5 The dux can also jump over a tile on to an empty square as shown. If your opponent's tile is then trapped between your dux and one of your tiles, his or her tile is captured.

During the game, you must move a tile or a dux if it is possible to do so – even if it means being captured. The winner is the first player to capture all of the other player's tiles and dux.

Chinese kite

The earliest kite flying in China was recorded during the Han Dynasty (206BC–AD220). These early kites were made of silk and bamboo. They were flown high in the sky during battles to scare off the enemy. Gradually, kites were flown during festivals. In the Qing Dynasty (1644–1912), a festival called Tengkao (Mounting the Height) was introduced by the Manchu emperors. People flew kites from high ground in the belief that this would bring them good luck.

Ever since ancient times, the Chinese have loved to play games and watch displays of martial arts and acrobatics. The nobility also invited acrobats and dancers into their homes to amuse their guests. Performances often lasted for hours, especially during festivals and ceremonies. Sports, such as polo and football, were also enjoyed by the wealthy. One emperor, Xuanzong, enjoyed polo so much that he failed to keep up with his official engagements.

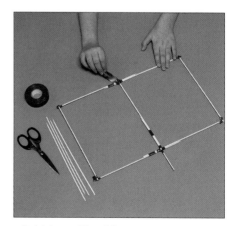

▲ Battleboard

The traditional game of xiang qi is similar to chess. One army battles against another, with round discs used as playing pieces. To tell the discs apart, each is marked with a name.

YOU WILL NEED

Thirteen barbecue sticks measuring 30cm long, ruler, PVA glue and glue brush, masking tape, scissors, white A1 paper, pencil, acrylic paints, paintbrush, water pot, 10m length of string, piece of wooden dowelling, small metal ring.

▲ Training for war
This figure shows an ancient Chinese polo player. Polo was originally played in India and Asia. It was invented as a training game to improve the riding skills of soldiers in cavalry units.

I Make a 40 x 30cm rectangle by gluing and taping sticks together. Overlap the sticks for strength. Join two sticks together to make a central rod that sticks out on one side as shown.

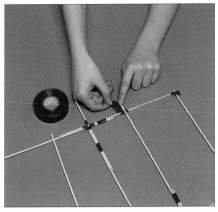

2 Use the last five sticks to make a rectangle measuring 40 x 15cm. Lay this rectangle on top of the first one at a right angle. Tape the two rectangles together as shown in steps 2 and 3.

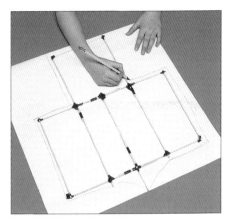

3 Place the frame on to a sheet of white A1 paper. Draw a border around the outside of the frame, 2.5cm out from the edge. Add curves around the end of the centre rod.

4 Cut out the kite shape you have drawn. Using a pencil, draw on the details of the dragon design shown in the final picture on this page. Paint in the design and leave it to dry.

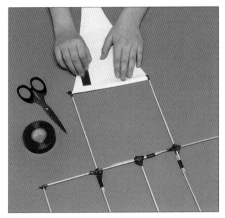

5 Cut a triangular piece of paper to make a tail for the end of your kite. Paint it and let it dry. Fold the tail over the rod at the bottom of the kite as shown. Tape the tail into position.

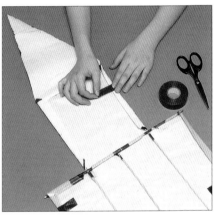

6 Carefully tape and glue your dragon design on to the frame of the kite. Fold the border over the frame and tape it on to the back of the kite as shown above.

7 Wrap the string round the dowelling and tie the end to a ring. Tie two pieces of string to the central rod of the frame. Make two holes in the kite, pass the strings through and tie to the ring.

Kites were invented in China around 3,000 years ago. They were often made into the shapes of animals or mythical creatures such as dragons. Today, Chinese children still play with home-made paper kites.

Japanese shell game

Perhaps one of the reasons why the Japanese invented the shell game was because shellfish have always been an important ingredient in Japanese food. Japan has a rich cultural history, and many pastimes have been handed down through the generations.

A game called menko, which has been played since the 1700s, involves throwing cards on the ground. Players try to flip their opponent's cards over by throwing their card on top of them. Karuta, another card game, has been popular since the 1600s. Karuta cards have pictures, words and poems written on them. In one version, known as iroha karuta, a player acts as the reader and keeps one set of karuta cards with sayings on them. The other players gather around a spread-out set of cards with the first letter or few words of the saying and a picture on them. When the reader starts reading a saying, the players try to find the matching karuta card. Whoever finds the card keeps it, and the player with the most cards at the end of the game wins.

▲ Counters from the sea
The Japanese often ate shellfish and kept the prettiest shells afterwards. They could then use them to play games such as this one.

YOU WILL NEED
Fresh clams, pan, water, bowl, selection of acrylic paints, paintbrush, water pot.

▲ Playing to win
Three court ladies play a card game, probably using karuta cards. These cards often included popular sayings from everyday Japanese life.

Ask an adult to boil the clams. Leave them to one side to cool and then remove the insides. Wash the shells and leave them to dry. When they are dry, paint the shells gold.

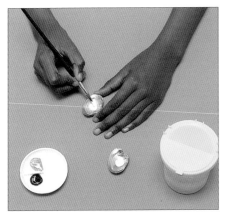

2 When the gold paint is dry, carefully pull each pair of shells apart. Then paint an identical design on to each shell of the pair. Start by painting a round, white face.

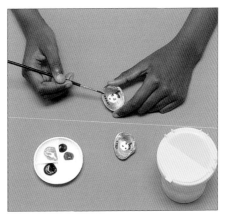

3 Add more features to the face, such as a mouth, hair and eyes. In the past, popular pictures, such as scenes from traditional stories, were painted on to the shell pairs.

4 Paint several pairs of clam shells with a variety of designs. Copy the ones here or make up your own. Make sure each pair of shells has an identical picture. Leave the painted shells to dry.

5 Now it is time to play the game. Turn all your shells face down and jumble them up. Turn over one shell and then challenge your opponent to pick the matching shell to yours.

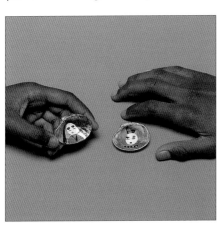

6 If the two shells do not match, turn them over and try again. If they do match, your opponent takes the shells. Take it in turns to challenge each other to find the matching pair.

The player with the most shells at the end of the game wins! Noble ladies at the imperial court enjoyed playing the shell game. This is a simplified version of the game they used to play.

Native American lacrosse

Between hunting expeditions and domestic tasks, Native Americans found time to relax and entertain themselves. Ball and stick games, such as lacrosse, were popular. There were also games of chance, gambling and tests of skill. Games of chance included guessing games, dice throwing and hand games where one person had to guess in which hand his opponent was hiding marked bones or wooden pieces. Archery, spear throwing and juggling were all fun to do and also helped to improve hunting skills.

Children loved to swim and take part in races. In the north, the girls and boys raced on toboggans. Active pastimes such as these helped to develop the skills a Native American needed to survive, such as strength, agility and stamina. Ritual foot races were also of ceremonial importance, helping the crops to grow, to bring rain and give renewed strength to the sun.

▲ **Twice the fun**
The ball game some Native Americans played used two sticks, although otherwise it was similar to lacrosse. The Cherokees called the game 'little brother of war'.

YOU WILL NEED

Thick card, ruler, pencil, scissors, masking tape, pair of compasses, barbecue stick, PVA glue and glue brush, bamboo stick (to reach your waist from ground level), string, brown paint, paintbrush, water pot, light ball.

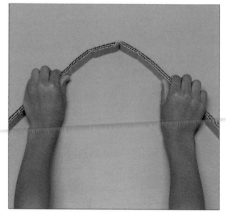

1 Measure and then cut a strip of card 120 x 3cm. Fold it gently at the centre to make a curve. You could also cut two pieces of card measuring 60 x 3cm and tape them together.

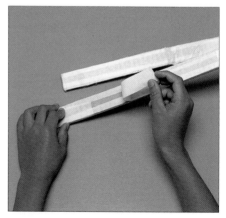

2 Completely cover the card strip with masking tape. Start from the edges and work your way around the strip, keeping the bent shape. Make sure you cover both sides of the card.

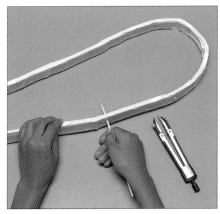

3 Use compasses to make two holes at the top of the bend, 10cm apart. Make two more holes 10cm from these and then two more 10cm further still. Enlarge with a barbecue stick.

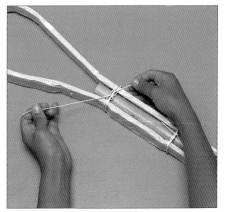

4 Glue the ends of the card strip to the top of the bamboo stick leaving a loop of card at the top as shown above. Tie a piece of string around the outside to keep it in place.

5 Pinch the card together where the loop meets the end of the stick. Tie it tightly with a piece of string, as shown above, and trim off the excess. Now paint the stick brown.

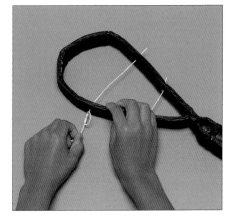

6 When the stick is dry, thread two pieces of string horizontally between the two sets of holes on the sides of the loop. Knot the pieces of string on the outside.

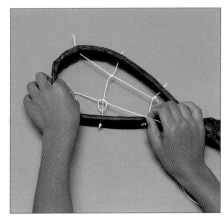

7 Now thread the vertical strings. Start at the holes at the top of the frame and tie the string around both horizontal strings. Tie the ends. Then try scooping up a ball with the stick.

The aim of the game of lacrosse is to get the leather ball between two posts to score a goal. It is a bit like hockey, but instead of hitting the ball, it is scooped up in the net of the stick.

Glossary

Assyrian An inhabitant of the Assyrian Empire. From 1530-612BC, Assyria occupied east of the Mediterranean Sea to Iran, and from the Persian Gulf to the mountains of eastern Turkey.

Aztec Mesoamerican people who lived in northern and central Mexico. The Aztecs were at their most powerful between 1350 and 1520.

B

bard A poet.

Before Christ (BC) A system used to calculate dates before the supposed year of Jesus Christ's birth. Dates are calculated in reverse. For example, 2000BC is longer ago than 200BC.

bonsai An ancient Japanese art of cultivating artificially miniaturized trees in small containers. The roots and shoots are pruned regularly, and wires are used to bend the branches to the desired shape.

Buddhism World religion founded in ancient India by the Buddha in the 6th century BC.

C

Celt A member of one of the ancient peoples that inhabited most parts of Europe from around 750BC to AD1000.

A

afterlife Life after death, as believed in by people of many world religions.

ancestor A member of the same family who died long ago.

Anno Domini (AD) A system used to calculate dates after the supposed year of Jesus Christ's birth. Anno Domini dates in this book are prefixed AD up to the year 1000, for example, AD521. After 1000 no prefixes are used.

archaeologist Someone who studies ancient ruins and artefacts to learn about the past.

archaeology The scientific study of the past, which involves looking at the remains of ancient civilizations.

artefact An object that has been preserved from the past.

civilization A society that makes advances in arts, sciences, law, technology and government.

cuneiform A type of writing that uses wedge-shaped figures, carved with a special tool. Cuneiform was developed by the Sumerians and also used by the Babylonians and Assyrians.

D

Dynasty A successive period of rule by generations of the same family.

E

Emperor The ruler of an empire

empire A group of lands ruled or governed by a single nation.

engrave To carve letters or designs on stone, wool or metal.

G

gem A precious or semi-precious stone or crystal, such as a diamond or ruby. Gems are often used to decorate jewellery or other garments.

H

Hinduism A world religion characterized by the worship of several gods and a belief in reincarnation.

I

ikebana The ancient Japanese art of flower arranging. Ikebana means 'living flowers'.

Inca A member of an indigenous South American civilization living in Peru before the Spanish conquest.

indigeous A person that is born in a particular area or country.

Islam A world religion founded in the 7th century AD by the prophet Mohammed.

K

kabuki A very popular and traditional form of Japanese drama where men play the roles of both males and females.

kendo A Japanese martial art that involves fighting with bamboo swords.

knucklebones A favourite game of the Greeks and Romans. Knucklebones involved flipping small animal bones from one side of the hand to another without dropping them.

M

megalith A large stone, either standing on its own or used as part of a tomb, stone circle or other monument.

Mesoamerica A geographical area made up of the land between Mexico and Panama in Central America.

Mesopotamia An ancient name for the fertile region between the Tigris and Euphrates rivers in the Middle East. This area is now occupied by Iraq.

Middle Ages Period in history that lasted from around AD800 to 1400.

missionary A member of a religious organization who carries out charitable work and religious teaching.

myth An ancient story that deals with gods and heroes.

N

Native Americans The indigenous peoples of the Americas.

nomads A group of people who roam from place to place in search of food or better land, or to follow herds.

P

patolli A popular board game played by the Aztecs.

pharoah A ruler of ancient Egypt.

R

ritual A procedure or series of actions often performed for a religious purpose.

S

Shinto An ancient Japanese faith known as the way of the gods and based on honouring holy spirits.

society All the classes of people living in a particular community or country.

shogun A Japanese army commander. Shoguns ruled Japan from 1185-1868.

shrine A place of worship or a container for holy relics such as bones.

Stone Age The first period in human history in which people made their tools and weapons out of stone.

V

Viking One of the Scandinavian peoples who lived by sea raiding in the early Middle Ages.

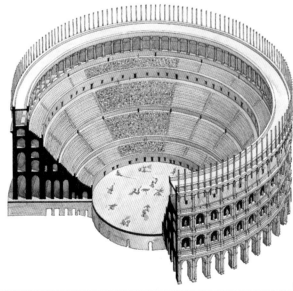

Index